Ultimate Sticker Collection

SUPERMAN™

DEADLY ENEMIES

HOW TO USE THIS BOOK

Read the captions, then find the sticker that best fits
in the space. (Hint: check the sticker labels for clues!)

•

Don't forget that your stickers can be
stuck down and peeled off again.

•

There are lots of fantastic extra stickers too!

DK

LONDON, NEW YORK,
MELBOURNE, MUNICH, AND DELHI

Written and edited by Catherine Saunders, Alastair Dougall, and Garima Sharma
Inside pages designed by Anamica Roy and Suzena Sengupta
Cover designed by Suzena Sengupta

Superman created by Jerry Siegel and Joe Shuster

First published in Great Britain in 2013 by
Dorling Kindersley Limited
80 Strand, London, WC2R 0RL
Penguin Group (UK)

10 9 8 7 6 5 4 3 2

002-184082-May/13

Page design copyright © 2013 Dorling Kindersley Limited.

A CIP catalogue record for this book is available from the British Library.

ISBN: 978-1-40932-894-0

Colour reproduction by Altaimage, UK
Printed and bound by L-Rex Pinting Co. Ltd, China

The following DC artists have contributed to this book: Oclair Albert, Marlo Alquiza, Brad Anderson, Mahmud Asrar, Mark Bagley,
Matt Banning, David Baron, Eddie Barrows, Moose Baumann Ed Benes, Patrick Blanc, Blond, BIT, Brian Buccellato, Marc Campos, Bernard Chang,
Cliff Chiang, Ian Churchill, Yildiray Cinar, David Curiel, Shane Davis, John Dell, Dale Eaglesham, Mark Farmer, Wayne Faucher, David Finch, Gary Frank,
Renato Guedes, Gene Ha, HI-FI, Sandra Hope, Richard Horie, Tanya Horie, J. G. Jones, Kano, Andy Kubert, Andy Lanning, Jim Lee, Rob Lean, Aaron Lopresti,
Art Lyon, Dave McCaig, Tom McCraw, Ed McGuinness, Mike McKone, J. P. Mayer, José Wilson Magalhaes, Francis Manapul, Doug Mahnke, Guy Major,
Jesús Merino, Rags Morales, Tom Nguyen, Carlos Pacheco, Jimmy Palmiotti, Pete Pantazis, Joe Phillips, Kilian Plunkett, Joe Prado, Mark Propst, Jay David
Ramos, Ivan Reis, Rod Reis, Alex Ross, Joe Rubinstein, Matt Ryan, Jesús Saiz, Nicola Scott, Steve Scott, Trevor Scott, Jon Sibal, R. B. Silva, Alex Sinclair,
Cam Smith, Ryan Sook, Dave Stewart, Rob Stull, Art Thibert, CAFU, Glenn Whitmore, Wildstorm FX, Scott Williams, Jason Wright, Pete Woods.

Discover more at
www.dk.com

Lex Luthor

Lex Luthor is the richest man in Metropolis and his business empire, LexCorp, employs a large portion of the city's inhabitants. He is also the most ruthless schemer in Metropolis and will stop at nothing to get what he wants. And what he wants most of all is to destroy Superman.

President Luthor
Lex can be charming when he needs to be. He pretended to approve of Superman in order to win votes and become President of the United States.

Damaged Child
Lex grew up in Smallville and knew Clark quite well. But after a lab accident in which he lost his hair, Lex became bitter and vengeful.

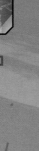

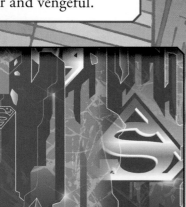

Battle Suit
Lex is no match for Superman in battle, so he created a special suit. It was made from impenetrable armour and equipped with deadly Kryptonite-powered weapons.

Injustice League
Lex formed a team of the world's greatest super-villains, including the Joker and Cheetah. Their mission was to conquer Earth and defeat the Justice League.

Infinity, Inc.
Lex acquired the technology to turn regular humans into super heroes. He created his own super hero team called Infinity, Inc. to carry out his orders.

Knocked Out
Even wearing his special battle suit, Lex Luthor was defeated by the Man of Steel.

Nice Try
Lex Luthor hoped to defeat Superman when he turned an ancient Kryptonian warship into a giant Kryptonite robot.

Revenge Squad
Lex Luthor's desire to destroy Superman and become the most powerful man in Metropolis led him to form the Superman Revenge Squad with villains Parasite, Metallo, and Bizarro.

Orange Lantern
A special power ring temporarily made Lex greedier than ever. He dreams of possessing the ring again, and becoming more powerful than Superman!

General Zod

Kryptonian villain General Zod tried to take over Krypton, and failed. His punishment was 40 years in the Phantom Zone, a prison outside space and time. As a result, Zod survived Krypton's destruction. When he was set free, Zod tried to conquer Earth.

Ursa

Zod's second-in-command, Ursa is almost as bad he is. She would do anything for her beloved general.

Military Man

On Krypton, Zod was a ruthless general. He is a skilled fighter and an expert in military tactics.

Phantom Zone

Prisoners in the Phantom Zone do not speak, eat, sleep, or grow older. They merely exist there until they have served their sentences.

Dangerous Foe

Zod was determined to take over Earth, but Superman defeated him and sent him back to where he belonged – in the Phantom Zone.

Brainiac

This evil alien is one of the most intelligent and dangerous beings in the universe. He travels through space looking for cities to shrink and store in bottles. Superman will never let Brainiac add Metropolis to his creepy collection.

Skull Ship

Brainiac roams the universe in a skull-shaped spaceship. He stores all his treasures on board and can connect his mind to the ship's core.

Collector of Worlds

Knowledge is power to Brainiac. He uses his ship to capture a planet's city, its people, and its culture in a bottle. Once done, he destroys the planet.

Brain Power

Brainiac is no fighter, but his mind is so powerful that he can control the actions of others. He took over Metallo to fight Superman.

Brainiac 13

This villain frequently upgrades his body. Brainiac 13 was so advanced that he travelled from the future to 21st-century Metropolis to take over Earth.

Ultimate Prize

Brainiac lured Superman aboard his ship hoping to fulfil his desire to add the Man of Steel to his collection of treasures.

Doomsday

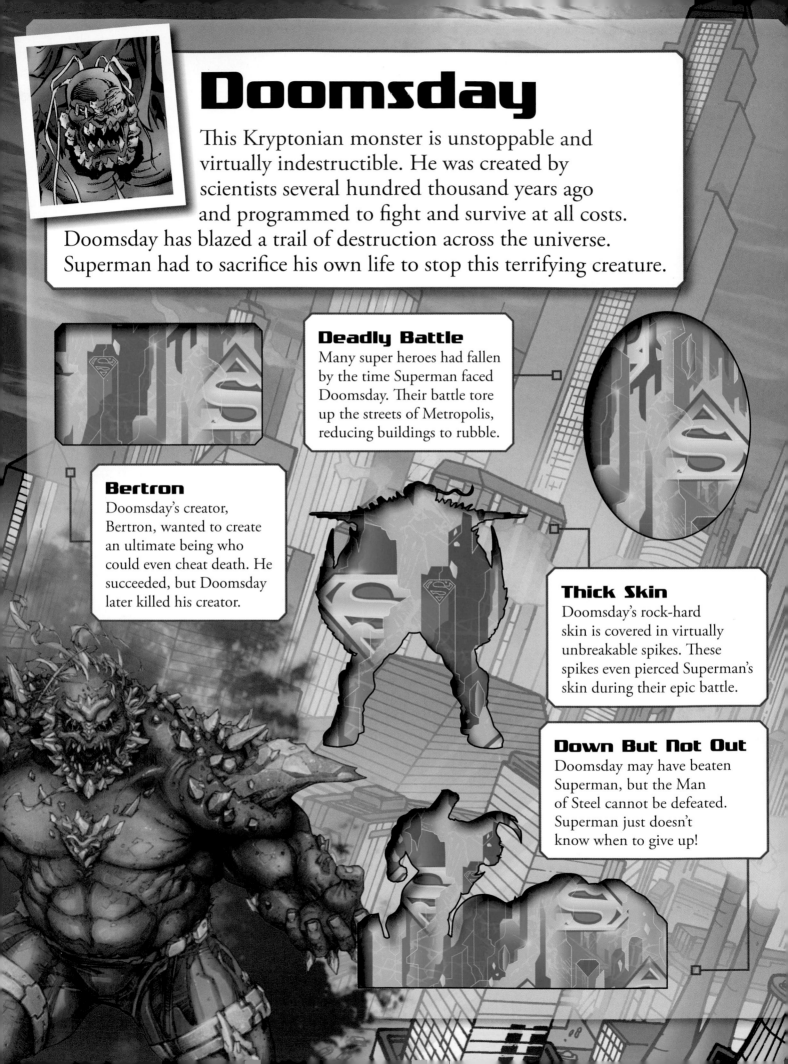

This Kryptonian monster is unstoppable and virtually indestructible. He was created by scientists several hundred thousand years ago and programmed to fight and survive at all costs. Doomsday has blazed a trail of destruction across the universe. Superman had to sacrifice his own life to stop this terrifying creature.

Deadly Battle

Many super heroes had fallen by the time Superman faced Doomsday. Their battle tore up the streets of Metropolis, reducing buildings to rubble.

Bertron

Doomsday's creator, Bertron, wanted to create an ultimate being who could even cheat death. He succeeded, but Doomsday later killed his creator.

Thick Skin

Doomsday's rock-hard skin is covered in virtually unbreakable spikes. These spikes even pierced Superman's skin during their epic battle.

Down But Not Out

Doomsday may have beaten Superman, but the Man of Steel cannot be defeated. Superman just doesn't know when to give up!

Darkseid

One of the universe's most powerful villains, Darkseid rules the planet Apokolips by fear. This tyrant seeks the legendary Anti-Life Equation, which would give him the power to enslave the whole universe. Superman will not let that happen!

Deadly Powers

Darkseid's body is practically impenetrable, and he is extremely intelligent. He can also read minds and move objects with his mind.

Apokolips

Darkseid's army of Parademons patrols the planet, hunting down anyone who defies his rule. The people of Apokolips are slaves known as the Hunger Dogs.

Omega Beams

Darkseid can project energy blasts, called Omega Beams, from his eyes. These can kill or transport a victim wherever Darkseid chooses.

Granny Goodness

Granny Goodness, Darkseid's evil minion, trains Darkseid's soldiers, turning them into brutal warriors who would die for their master.

Alien Foes

Earth has had many visitors, not all of them welcome. Some of the Man of Steel's greatest challenges have come from evil aliens. While some plan to invade and conquer the planet, others just want to cause trouble. Whatever their evil plans, it's Superman's job to try and stop them.

H'el
This powerful Kryptonian explorer believes that Earthlings are unworthy of Superman and sees himself as the ultimate protector of Kryptonian culture.

Replikon

First, Replikon tried to destroy life on Earth, and failed. He then tried to defeat Superman, but he failed at that, too.

Lobo
Unlike Superman, this superpowered bounty hunter doesn't care about right or wrong. He hires himself out for money and never gives up until the job is done.

Auctioneer
This powerful being collects and sells the universe's most interesting things to the highest bidder. The Man of Steel is high on his list.

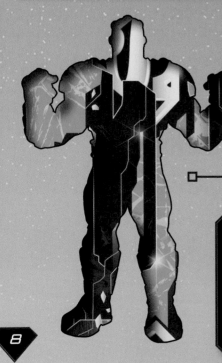

Mongul

He travelled the cosmos on his planet-sized base, Warworld, but the super-strong Mongul proved no match for Superman.

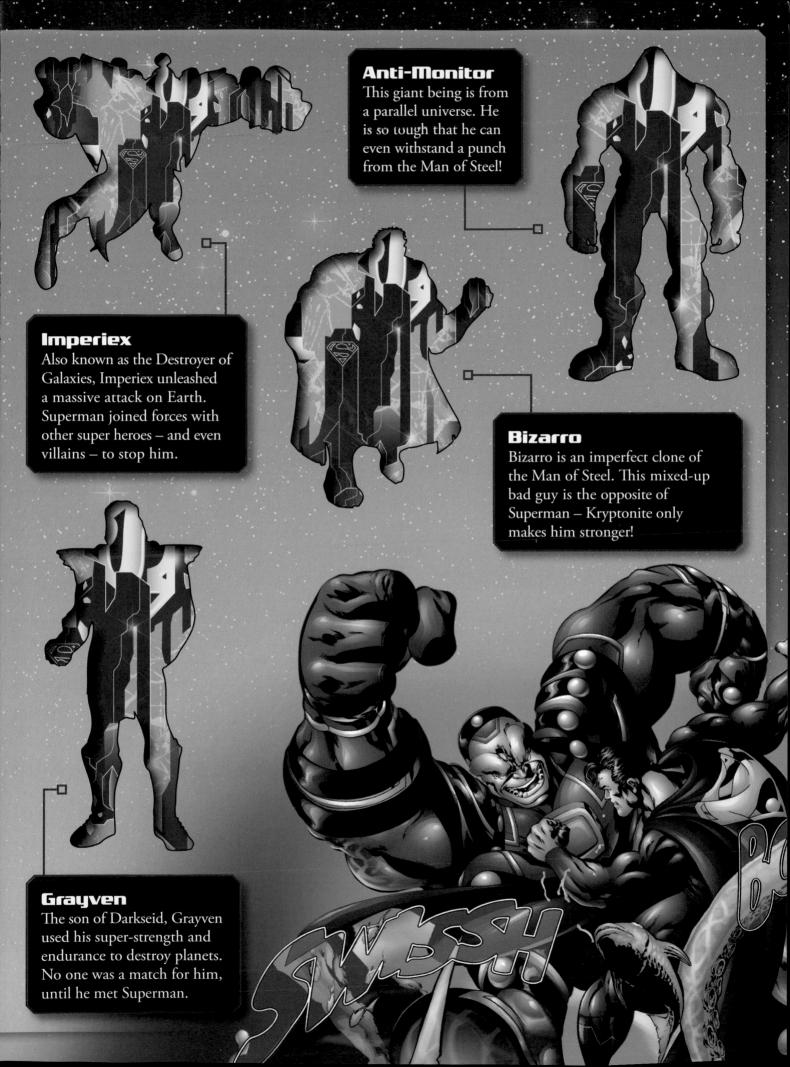

Anti-Monitor
This giant being is from a parallel universe. He is so tough that he can even withstand a punch from the Man of Steel!

Imperiex
Also known as the Destroyer of Galaxies, Imperiex unleashed a massive attack on Earth. Superman joined forces with other super heroes – and even villains – to stop him.

Bizarro
Bizarro is an imperfect clone of the Man of Steel. This mixed-up bad guy is the opposite of Superman – Kryptonite only makes him stronger!

Grayven
The son of Darkseid, Grayven used his super-strength and endurance to destroy planets. No one was a match for him, until he met Superman.

Parasite

Rudy Jones wanted more out of life, but he got more than he bargained for when he ate a doughnut covered in toxic waste. Jones was transformed into a greedy, power-absorbing villain named Parasite. This hideous monster is hungry for power – making Superman his primary target.

Monster Looks

Parasite is not a pretty sight. He has a blubbery body and a mouth full of sharp teeth that fasten onto his prey.

Power Thief

Parasite is hungry for Superman's powers. He's come close, but so far hasn't been able to combat the Man of Steel's abilities.

Greedy

Parasite only has to touch someone to absorb their powers. He can even assume their shape and personality.

Warming Up

When Supergirl faced Parasite, the evil monster absorbed all her abilities.

Metallo

John Corben was an ordinary soldier in the US Army, until he underwent a top-secret military procedure. The experiment's real aim was to create a soldier who could defeat Superman, and it was funded by Superman's richest and most devious foe, Lex Luthor.

New Man

Corben became part human, part robot. The experiment also made his heart burst, so Luthor gave him a new one – made of Kryptonite.

Heart to Kill

Superman is more than a match for Metallo – until the villain reveals his Kryptonite heart and weakens the Man of Steel.

Getting Ahead

Superman once prevented Metallo from causing mayhem by destroying his body and removing his head!

Deadly Mission

Every time Metallo is defeated, he simply repairs his metallic body to continue his rampages.

Other Foes

It's not just visitors from other worlds who cause problems for Superman, Earth has some pretty bad people, too. Many of them seem to really dislike the Man of Steel – he's always getting in their way, thwarting their evil plans, and protecting the people of Earth.

Livewire
Leslie Lewis became super-villain Livewire after losing her job. Born with the gift of manipulating electricity, her lightning blasts can stun Superman.

Cyborg Superman
A failed space mission turned Hank Henshaw into a cyborg. He once pretended to be a super hero to make Superman look bad.

Manchester Black
He hated Superman for his belief in honour and justice, and tried to use his psychic powers against the Man of Steel.

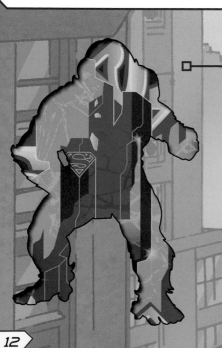

Ultra-Humanite
To save his powerful brain from his failing body, Ultra-Humanite began transferring his brain into powerful bodies – such as that of a large white gorilla

Bruno Mannheim
The head of Metropolis's Intergang, this powerful criminal recently joined forces with the evil alien Darkseid.

Conduit

Radiation from the rocket that brought Superman to Earth gave Kenny Braverman superpowers. As Conduit, he channelled those powers through a high-tech battlesuit.

Atomic Skull

An alien "gene bomb" made Joe Martin invisible. It also made him crazy – he thinks Superman is a villain!

Prankster

Oswald Loomis, an ex-TV star, is famous for all the wrong reasons as the villainous Prankster.

Toyman

The toys he creates are deadly. No one was safe when Toyman unleashed his army of Superman toys in Metropolis.

Maxwell Lord

Maxwell Lord once controlled Superman's mind. Fortunately, Wonder Woman saved the Man of Steel.

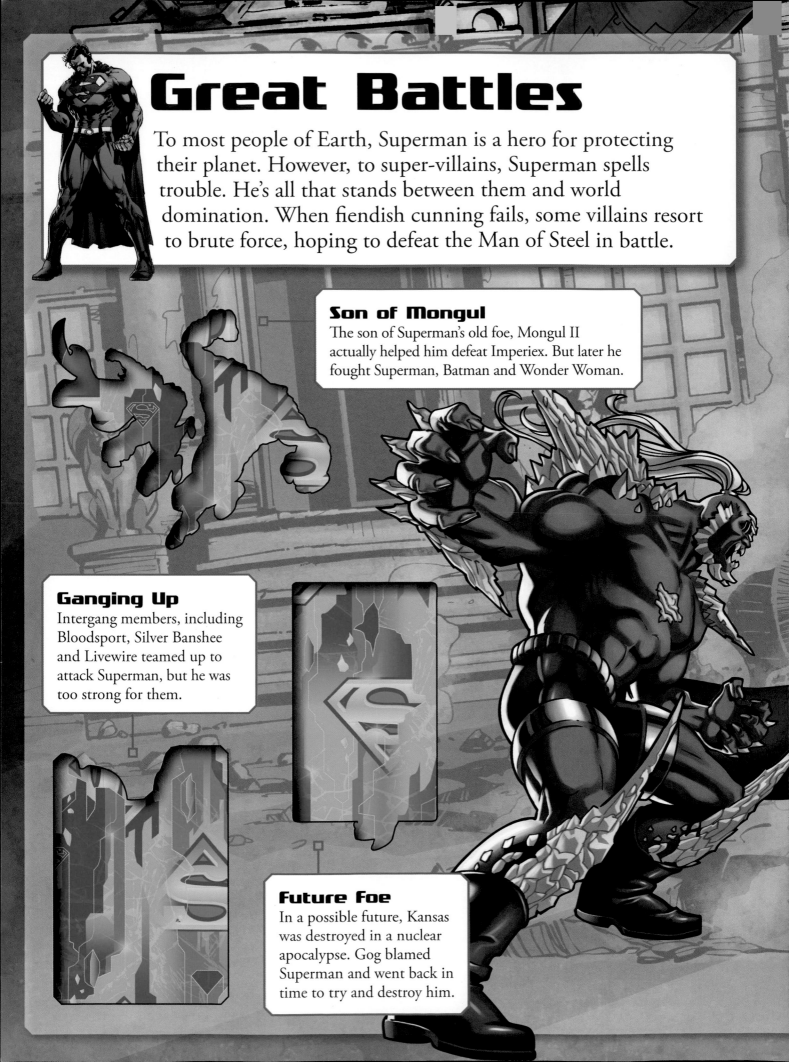

Great Battles

To most people of Earth, Superman is a hero for protecting their planet. However, to super-villains, Superman spells trouble. He's all that stands between them and world domination. When fiendish cunning fails, some villains resort to brute force, hoping to defeat the Man of Steel in battle.

Son of Mongul

The son of Superman's old foe, Mongul II actually helped him defeat Imperiex. But later he fought Superman, Batman and Wonder Woman.

Ganging Up

Intergang members, including Bloodsport, Silver Banshee and Livewire teamed up to attack Superman, but he was too strong for them.

Future Foe

In a possible future, Kansas was destroyed in a nuclear apocalypse. Gog blamed Superman and went back in time to try and destroy him.

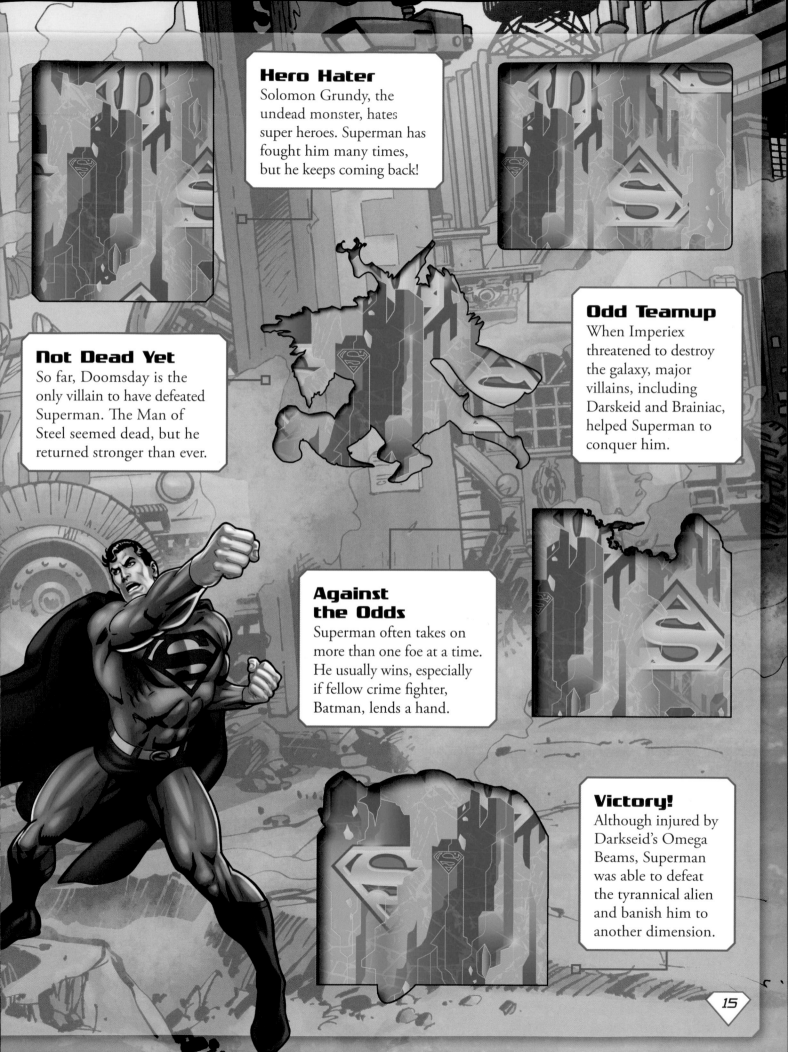

Hero Hater
Solomon Grundy, the undead monster, hates super heroes. Superman has fought him many times, but he keeps coming back!

Not Dead Yet
So far, Doomsday is the only villain to have defeated Superman. The Man of Steel seemed dead, but he returned stronger than ever.

Odd Teamup
When Imperiex threatened to destroy the galaxy, major villains, including Darskeid and Brainiac, helped Superman to conquer him.

Against the Odds
Superman often takes on more than one foe at a time. He usually wins, especially if fellow crime fighter, Batman, lends a hand.

Victory!
Although injured by Darkseid's Omega Beams, Superman was able to defeat the tyrannical alien and banish him to another dimension.

Magic Villains

Despite his awesome abilities, Superman has a surprising weakness – magic. The Man of Steel can be affected by magical forces, and he has no power over the supernatural. Superman can't explain why – there are no logical explanations when magic is involved!

Mr. Mxyzptlk
This mischievous imp from the Fifth Dimension torments Superman with his magic. The Man of Steel does not find his practical jokes funny!

Eclipso
Using his magical black diamond, Eclipso once controlled Superman and made him attack the hero Shazam.

Encantadora
This troublesome enchantress gave Superman a Kryptonite kiss, nearly killing him. She then sold fake Kryptonite to Superman's enemies.

Black Adam
Black Adam is an ancient Egyptian prince with magical powers, who has clashed with Superman in the past.

Silver Banshee
Her high-pitched screams are deadly for humans. But Silver Banshee is equally dangerous to Kryptonians, too. She once turned Supergirl into a Banshee!

Stickers

Replikon

Thick Skin

Victory!

Grayven

Battle Suit

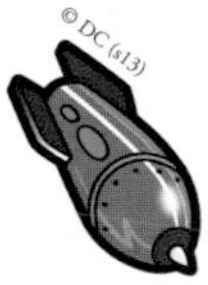

Getting Ahead

Apokolips

Mr. Mxyzptlk

Lobo

Stickers

Imperiex

Not Dead Yet

Bruno Mannheim

Bizarro

Future Foe

Deadly Battle

Revenge Squad

Knocked Out

Manchester Black

Stickers

Greedy

Odd Teamup

Warming Up

Son of Mongul

Military
Man

Cyborg
Superman

Granny Goodness

Heart to Kill

Ultimate Prize

Black Adam

Stickers

Against the Odds

Orange Lantern

Auctioneer

Mongul

Atomic Skull

President Luthor

Conduit

Omega Beams

Power Thief

Stickers

H'el

Toyman

Nice Try

Skull Ship

Injustice League

New Man

Livewire

Eclipso

Anti-Monitor

Stickers

Infinity, Inc.

Phantom Zone

Prankster

Deadly Powers

Collector of Worlds

Monster Looks

Brain Power

Silver Banshee

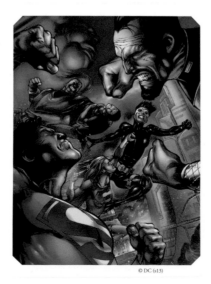

Dangerous Foe

Damaged Child

Stickers

Hero Hater

Deadly Mission

Ultra-Humanite

Maxwell Lord

Bertron

Brainiac 13

Encantadora

Down But Not Out

Ursa

Ganging Up

Stickers